calf

udder

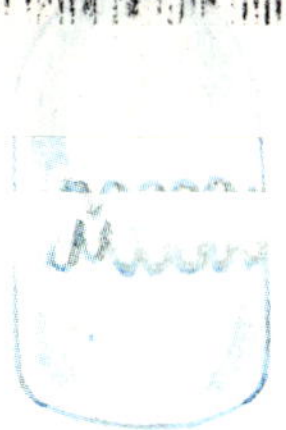

milk

cowshed

foal

mane

saddle

stable

lamb

ram

wool

shepherd

kid

beard

cheese

post

Published in the UK in 1994 by Schofield & Sims Limited, Huddersfield, England.

0 7217 5022 2

PLAY WORDS

On the Farm

SCHOFIELD & SIMS LIMITED, HUDDERSFIELD, ENGLAND

chicks

eggs

cockerel

fox

The hen 

The  and her  peck for food in the farmyard. The farmer collects the  that the  has laid. The  crows every morning. The hens sleep in the hen-house every night because the  is prowling about. The  is his favourite food.

young rabbits

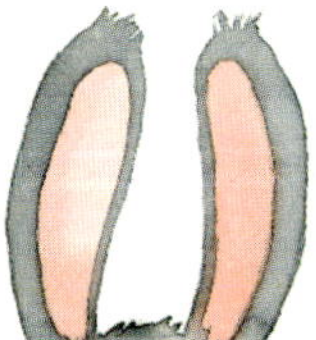

ears

hutch

carrots

The rabbit 

The farmer keeps the  and its young ones in a  . The  are very soft and fluffy. They have very big  like their parents.

In his basket, the farmer is carrying some  . What luck!  love to eat  .

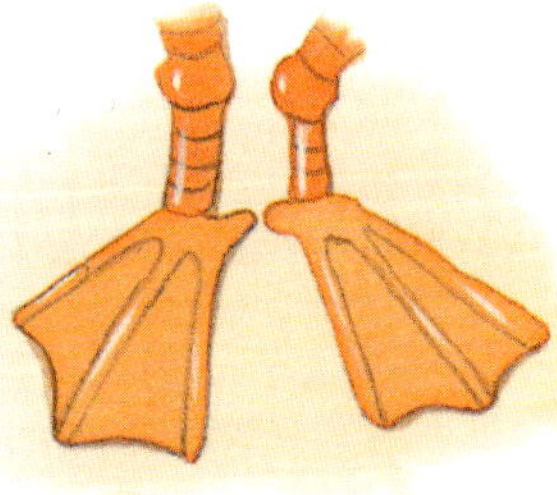

ducklings webbed feet swim pond

The duck 

The  loves playing in the water. She has  that allow her to  very quickly. The little  paddle in the  while their mother watches them. The  are hungry and love the bread that children throw to them in the  .

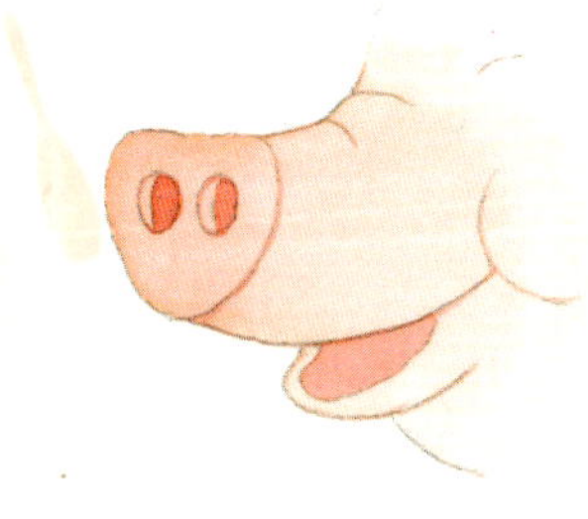

piglets snout curly tail mud

The pig 

The  eats everything. It scrapes the soil using its 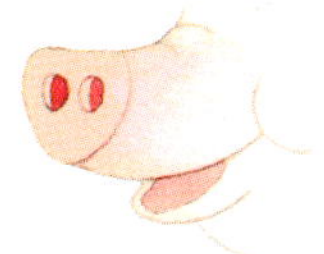 to look for food. The  gets dirty because it loves rolling in the  . Young pigs are called  . Their mother, the sow, suckles them. They have a  .

calf

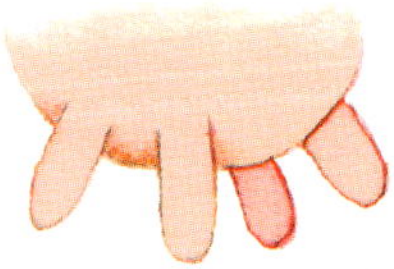

udder

milk

cowshed

The cow

The  eats grass, then she makes 

. Every morning and evening, when the cow's 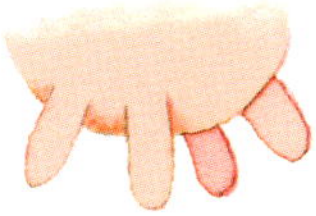 is full, the farmer milks her. The little  drinks the 

of its mother when it suckles. Each night, the  sleeps next to the  in the  .

foal

mane

saddle

stable

The horse 

The  grazes in the field with its little . The farmer sometimes puts a  on the back of the , and sets off to ride in the countryside. When the  gallops, its  streams in the wind. At night, the  sleeps in a .

lamb

ram

wool

shepherd

The sheep 

The  looks after the flock in the field. The  eats a lot of grass. The young  is called a . It has a soft coat. The father has horns and is called a . In summer, the  shears the  so we can have .

kid

beard

cheese

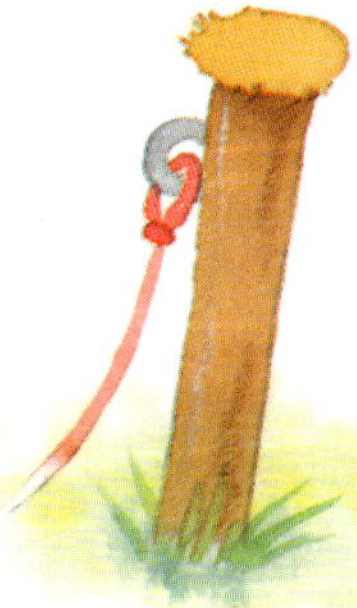

post

The nanny-goat 

The  is tied to a  .

She grazes on grass. The young  is called a  . The  leaps up and down. Its father, the billy-goat, has a  . Every day, the farmer milks the  . With the milk, he makes delicious  .

chicks

eggs

cockerel

fox

young rabbits

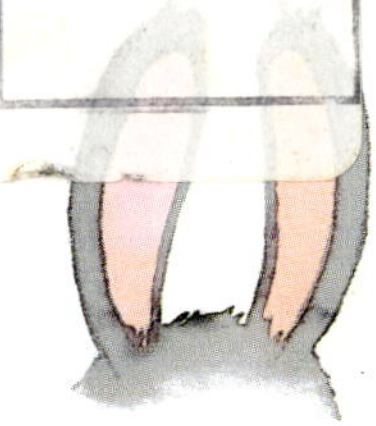

ears

hutch

carrots

ducklings

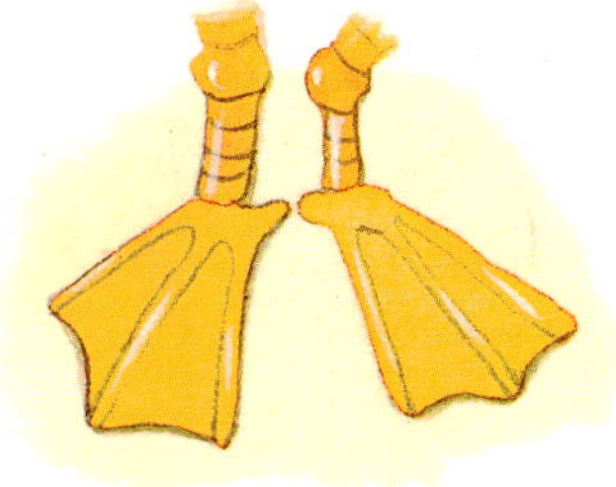

webbed feet

swim

pond

piglets

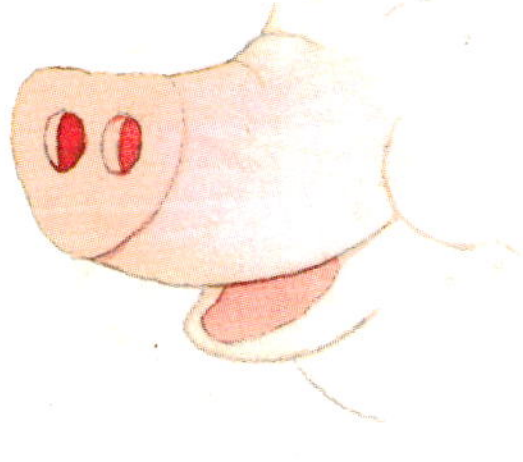

snout

curly tail

mud